TESTS AND Teaching Quality

Interim Report

Committee on Assessment and Teacher Quality

Board on Testing and Assessment

National Research Council

NATIONAL ACADEMY PRESS
Washington, DC

NATIONAL ACADEMY PRESS • 2101 Constitution Avenue, NW • Washington, DC 20418

NOTICE: The project that is the subject of this report was approved by the Governing Board of the National Research Council, whose members are drawn from the councils of the National Academy of Sciences, the National Academy of Engineering, and the Institute of Medicine. The members of the committee responsible for the report were chosen for their special competences and with regard for appropriate balance.

The study was supported by U.S. Department of Education (award R215U990004). Any opinions, findings, conclusions, or recommendations expressed in this publication are those of the author(s) and do not necessarily reflect the view of the organizations or agencies that provided support for this project.

International Standard Book Number 0-309-06946-7

Additional copies of this report are available from:

National Academy Press
2101 Constitution Avenue, NW
Washington, DC 20418

Call (800) 624-6242 or (202) 334-3313 (in the Washington metropolitan area). This report is also available online at http://www.nap.edu

Suggested citation: National Research Council (2000) *Tests and Teaching Quality: Interim Report*. Committee on Assessment and Teaching Quality, Board on Testing and Assessment. Washington, DC: National Academy Press.

Printed in the United States of America

Copyright 2000 by the National Academy of Sciences. All rights reserved.

THE NATIONAL ACADEMIES

National Academy of Sciences
National Academy of Engineering
Institute of Medicine
National Research Council

The **National Academy of Sciences** is a private, nonprofit, self-perpetuating society of distinguished scholars engaged in scientific and engineering research, dedicated to the furtherance of science and technology and to their use for the general welfare. Upon the authority of the charter granted to it by the Congress in 1863, the Academy has a mandate that requires it to advise the federal government on scientific and technical matters. Dr. Bruce M. Alberts is president of the National Academy of Sciences.

The **National Academy of Engineering** was established in 1964, under the charter of the National Academy of Sciences, as a parallel organization of outstanding engineers. It is autonomous in its administration and in the selection of its members, sharing with the National Academy of Sciences the responsibility for advising the federal government. The National Academy of Engineering also sponsors engineering programs aimed at meeting national needs, encourages education and research, and recognizes the superior achievements of engineers. Dr. William A. Wulf is president of the National Academy of Engineering.

The **Institute of Medicine** was established in 1970 by the National Academy of Sciences to secure the services of eminent members of appropriate professions in the examination of policy matters pertaining to the health of the public. The Institute acts under the responsibility given to the National Academy of Sciences by its congressional charter to be an adviser to the federal government and, upon its own initiative, to identify issues of medical care, research, and education. Dr. Kenneth I. Shine is president of the Institute of Medicine.

The **National Research Council** was organized by the National Academy of Sciences in 1916 to associate the broad community of science and technology with the Academy's purposes of furthering knowledge and advising the federal government. Functioning in accordance with general policies determined by the Academy, the Council has become the principal operating agency of both the National Academy of Sciences and the National Academy of Engineering in providing services to the government, the public, and the scientific and engineering communities. The Council is administered jointly by both Academies and the Institute of Medicine. Dr. Bruce M. Alberts and Dr. William A. Wulf are chairman and vice chairman, respectively, of the National Research Council.

COMMITTEE ON ASSESSMENT AND TEACHER QUALITY

DAVID Z. ROBINSON (*Chair*), Carnegie Corporation of New York
ANDY BAUMGARTNER, William Robinson Center, Augusta, GA
JOHN T. BRUER, James S. McDonnell Foundation, St. Louis, MO
CARL A. GRANT, Department of Teacher Education, University of Wisconsin-Madison
MILTON D. HAKEL, Department of Psychology, Bowling Green State University
LINDA DARLING-HAMMOND, School of Education, Stanford University
ABIGAIL L. HUGHES, Connecticut State Department of Education
MARY M. KENNEDY, College of Education, Michigan State University
STEPHEN P. KLEIN, RAND, Santa Monica, CA
KATE MANSKI, Department of English, University of Illinois-Chicago
C. FORD MORISHITA, Clackamas High School, Milwaukie, OR
PAMELA A. MOSS, Department of Education, University of Michigan
BARBARA STERRETT PLAKE, Buros Institute of Mental Measurements, University of Nebraska-Lincoln
DAVID L. ROSE, Rose and Rose, Attorneys at Law, Washington, DC
PORTIA HOLMES SHIELDS, Ofice of the President, Albany State University
JAMES STIGLER, Psychology Department, University of California, Los Angeles
KEN I. WOLPIN, Department of Economics, University of Pennsylvania

ROBERT ROTHMAN, *Study Director*
KAREN MITCHELL, *Senior Program Officer*
KAELI KNOWLES, *Program Officer*
DOROTHY MAJEWSKI, *Senior Project Assistant*

BOARD ON TESTING AND ASSESSMENT

ROBERT L. LINN *(Chair)*, School of Education, University of Colorado, Boulder
CARL F. KAESTLE *(Vice Chair)*, Department of Education, Brown University
RICHARD C. ATKINSON, President, University of California
PAUL J. BLACK, School of Education, King's College, London, England
RICHARD P. DURÁN, Graduate School of Education, University of California, Santa Barbara
CHRISTOPHER F. EDLEY, JR., Harvard Law School, Harvard University
RONALD FERGUSON, John F. Kennedy School of Public Policy, Harvard University
ROBERT M. HAUSER, Institute for Research on Poverty, University of Wisconsin
PAUL W. HOLLAND, Graduate School of Education, University of California, Berkeley
RICHARD M. JAEGER, Center for Educational Research and Evaluation, University of North Carolina
BARBARA M. MEANS, SRI International, Menlo Park, CA
LORRAINE MCDONNELL, Department of Political Science, University of California, Santa Barbara
KENNETH PEARLMAN, Lucent Technologies, Inc., Warren, NJ
ANDREW C. PORTER, Wisconsin Center for Education Research, University of Wisconsin, Madison
CATHERINE E. SNOW, Graduate School of Education, Harvard University
WILLIAM L. TAYLOR, Attorney at Law, Washington, DC
WILLIAM T. TRENT, Associate Chancellor, University of Illinois, Champaign
VICKI VANDAVEER, The Vandaveer Group, Inc., Houston, TX
LAURESS L. WISE, Human Resources Research Organization, Alexandria, VA
KENNETH I. WOLPIN, Department of Economics, University of Pennsylvania

MICHAEL J. FEUER, *Director*
VIOLA C. HOREK, *Administrative Associate*
LISA ALSTON, *Administrative Assistant*

Acknowledgments

This report benefited from the insights and support of a number of people, and the committee is grateful for their contributions. We want first of all to acknowledge our sponsors, who made the project possible and kept it going. At the U.S. Department of Education, Terry K. Dozier backed the project enthusiastically and made it a priority at the department. Thelma Leenhouts showed a continuing interest in the project and kept us apprised of events and publications that would assist us in our work.

The committee was also aided greatly by individuals who participated in our meetings and helped us understand the complex issues involved in teacher licensure testing. Carolyn Maidon of the North Carolina Department of Public Instruction, Maureen Carvan of the Ohio Department of Education, Pat Glenn of the Illinois Department of Education, and Raymond Pecheone of the Connecticut State Department of Education provided information about their states' systems for licensing teachers, and Drew Gitomer of the Educational Testing Service, Richard Allan of National Evaluation Systems Inc., and Jean Miller of the Interstate New Teachers Assessment and Support Consortium helped us understand the role of testing organizations.

At our third meeting, a panel of recent graduates from Albany State University—Joycelyn Hagans, Tesharra Starling, and VaShaun Harper—described for us their experience as test takers. Joan Baratz-Snowden of the American Federation of Teachers and Nesa Chappelle of the National Education Association discussed testing issues from the perspective of their memberships.

The committee also commissioned several papers to provide a range of perspectives on criteria for evaluating licensure systems. Linda Crocker of the University of Florida, Mary Hatwood Futrell of George Washington University, Dan Goldhaber of the Urban Institute, Richard Jaeger of the University of North Carolina-Greensboro, P. Richard Jeanneret of Jeanneret and Associates, and Diana Pullin of Boston University were generous in sharing their thoughts and research on the issues involved.

Within the National Research Council, a number of individuals helped us keep the project moving forward. Barbara Boyle Torrey, executive director of the Commission on Behavioral and Social Sciences and Education, enthusiastically backed the project and lent us her wisdom and advice at key stages. Michael J. Feuer, director of the Board on Testing and Assessment, was a guiding force behind the project and provided substantive advice and moral support throughout the process. Eugenia Grohman's skillful editing was indispensible, and her knowledge and experience guided us through the NRC's report review process.

The committee's staff worked extremely hard and skillfully to enable us to produce this report. Robert Rothman, Karen Mitchell, and Kaeli Knowles helped ensure that the meetings were informative and productive, and developed numerous drafts and revisions. Dorothy Majewski, the senior project assistant, handled the logistics of our work with dexterity and good humor.

This report has been reviewed in draft form by individuals chosen for their diverse perspectives and technical expertise, in accordance with procedures approved by the NRC's Report Review Committee. The purpose of this independent review is to provide candid and critical comments that will assist the institution in making the published report as sound as possible and to ensure that the report meets institutional standards for objectivity, evidence, and responsiveness to the study charge. The review comments and draft manuscript remain confidential to protect the integrity of the deliberative process.

We wish to thank the following individuals for their participation in the review of this report: Edward Haertel, School of Education, Stanford University; Robert Hauser, Center for Demography, University of Wisconsin-Madison; Henry M. Levin, Departments of Economics and Education, Teachers College, Columbia University; Robert L. Linn, School of Education, University of Colorado, Boulder; Duncan Luce, Institute for Mathematical Behavioral Science, University of California, Irvine; Carolyn Morse, Department of Chemistry, University of North Carolina; Richard Murnane, Graduate School of Education, Harvard University; Edward Rossiter, Newton North High School, Newton, MA; and Paul Sackett, Department of Psychology, University of Minnesota.

Although these individuals provided many constructive comments and suggestions, responsibility for the final content of this report rests solely with the authoring committee and the institution.

David Z. Robinson, *Chair*
Committee on Assessment and Teacher Quality

Contents

Executive Summary	1
Introduction	4
Current Licensure Testing	6
The Development and Quality of Licensure Tests	13
Disparate Impact	17
Conclusions	19
Appendix	21
References	29
Bibliography	31
Biographical Sketches	37

Executive Summary

Improving the quality of teaching in elementary and secondary schools is now high on the nation's educational policy agenda. Policy makers at the state and federal levels have focused on initiatives designed to improve the abilities of teachers already in schools and increase the numbers of well-qualified teachers available to fill current and future vacancies.

As part of their efforts, many policy makers have prescribed tests as a measure of the quality of teachers and teaching, and there is strong interest in requiring teachers to pass a test to earn a license. Moreover, Congress and the President have raised the profile of licensure tests by requiring states and institutions of higher education to report passing rates on such tests.

In response to the increased interest in tests for teachers, the U.S. Department of Education asked the National Research Council (NRC) to study the issue. The NRC convened the Committee on Assessment and Teacher Quality, which has begun a 20-month investigation of the technical, educational, and legal issues surrounding the use of tests for licensing teachers. This interim report covers the first nine months of the committee's study and focuses on existing tests and their use.

The purpose of licensure is to protect the public from harm by setting minimal qualifications for beginning practitioners. To license teachers, states seek a variety of evidence that candidates possess such qualifications, including coursework in state-approved teacher education programs at the undergraduate or graduate level, a major or minor in the intended teaching field, and student-teaching experience. Forty-one states require prospective teachers to pass one or more tests.

States vary considerably in what they test, how they test it, and the level of performance they require for passing. Some states use examinations that assess basic skills, while others assess subject-area knowledge, pedagogical knowledge and skills, or a combination of these types of measures. Test format also varies. Some exams rely on multiple-choice items; others use open-ended questions or a combination of these or other formats (such as portfolios or more performance-based measures). Even when states use the same test, they set different scores for passing.

As a result of these differences in testing practices and standards, it is not feasible to make meaningful comparisons in passing rates among states. At the institutional level, there are variations in policies regarding who is admitted to and graduated from teacher education programs and when these programs require or allow candidates to take the tests. Thus comparisons of passing rates among institutions are difficult to interpret as well.

While licensure policies and testing requirements are intended to set minimal qualifications for public school teachers, two-thirds of the states allow waivers from state licensure requirements for one or more tests. Waivers allow districts to fill vacancies when not enough licensed teachers are available. As a result, classrooms may have teachers who have not satisfied all of their state's testing requirements. In some states, the numbers of teachers with such waivers is substantial.

To construct a licensure test, test developers often begin by collecting data, which ranges from the solicitation of informed judgment to conducting formal surveys, and conducting an analysis to determine the knowledge and skills that a minimally qualified beginning teacher would need. These determinations vary from state to state. Once the test is developed, states set passing scores. Typically, the passing score is based on recommendations from panels of educators who are asked to estimate the level of performance on the test a minimally qualified candidate would be expected to achieve.

Most of the validity evidence currently available for teacher licensure tests is based on judgments about whether the test is likely to assess the knowledge and skills it was intended to measure and whether such knowledge and skills are necessary for beginning teachers to possess. This evidence helps indicate test quality and helps assure policy makers and the public that the test results indicate that teachers are likely to possess the knowledge and skills judged necessary for teaching. However, some tests have been criticized for failing to adhere to professional guidelines for development and validation.

The information licensure tests provide may be deemed necessary, but it is not sufficient to determine whether teachers will be effective in the classroom. Currently, there is little research on the relationship between teachers' test scores and their teaching performance. Such research is difficult to conduct, but it is important. Such research would provide a better understanding of what teacher licensure tests measure.

Even under the best of circumstances, teacher licensure tests, like tests for other professions, cannot be expected to measure everything that is important for practice. Good teachers can explain ideas in ways that different students understand; they are compassionate, resourceful, committed, honest, and persistent in their efforts to help children learn. All of these things are important to teaching, but difficult to measure. A single test or set of tests can only measure some of the characteristics associated with competent teaching.

Blacks and Hispanics generally earn lower scores than whites on licensure tests for teachers. Consequently, blacks and Hispanics tend to have lower passing rates. The same is true for licensing tests in other professions. The disparities in passing scores have contributed to problems faced by schools that want to hire a diverse teaching force and have led to legal challenges. Evidence is needed to determine whether the disparities in average scores and passing rates among groups on these tests are due to actual differences in mastery of the knowledge and skills the tests were designed to assess rather than something else.

As a result of its preliminary explorations and discussions, the committee has reached five conclusions:

- Licensure tests are designed to provide useful information about the extent to which prospective teachers possess the literacy and mathematics skills and/or the subject-matter and pedagogical knowledge that states consider necessary for beginning teaching.
- Teacher licensure tests assess only some of the characteristics that are deemed to be important for effective practice. They are not designed to predict who will become effective teachers.
- There is currently little evidence available about the extent to which widely used teacher licensure tests distinguish between candidates who are minimally competent to teach and those who are not.
- Comparisons of passing rates among states are not useful for policy purposes because of the diversity of testing and licensure practices.
- Test instruments, pass/fail rules, and other licensing requirements and policies that result in large differences in eventual passing rates among racial/ethnic groups pose problems for schools that seek to have a diverse teaching force.

Introduction

As policy makers at the federal and state levels have moved in numerous ways over the past two decades to adopt reforms in education, one focus has been on the initial licensure of teachers. In particular, many states have increased the educational and academic requirements for prospective teachers, set new standards for approval of teacher education institutions, and added requirements that teachers demonstrate evidence of subject-matter knowledge or understanding of teaching and learning. A few states have incorporated the assessment of teachers' classroom performance as a component of their complete licensure process.

Many policy makers have prescribed tests to measure the quality of teachers and teaching. The number of states requiring testing for entry into the teaching profession increased from 3 in 1977 to 44 in 1987. Currently, 41 states require tests for licensure, and some of the remaining states are considering adding such requirements.

The interest in testing teachers reflects Americans' historical faith in testing and skepticism about other methods of determining quality (Haney et al., 1987). At the same time, teacher licensure tests have been strongly criticized. Critics have charged that many of the tests fail to measure critical knowledge and skills in effective ways and that the use of inadequate tests may inappropriately affect the supply of well-qualified teachers and the preparation future teachers receive (Haertel, 1991; National Commission on Teaching and America's Future, 1996; Darling-Hammond et al., 1999).

The federal government recently raised the profile of licensure tests. Under the Higher Education Amendments of 1998 (P.L. 105-244), states are required to report the assessments used for licensing teachers, the standards that teacher-candidates must meet in order to earn a license, and the pass rates on such tests for the graduates of each institution that educates teachers. The law also requires institutions to publish a "report card" that must include, among other information, pass rates on teacher licensure tests and a comparison of the institutional rates with state averages. Sponsors of the measure said that they intended it to hold teacher education institutions accountable for the education of prospective teachers.

In the midst of this interest in testing and initiatives at the federal and state levels, the U.S. Department of Education asked the National Research Council (NRC) to study teacher testing. The Committee on Assessment and Teacher Quality was charged with providing guidance to the department and the states in analyzing and revising their systems for the initial licensure of teachers. This interim report covers the first 9 months of the committee's 20-month study.

The committee interpreted its charge to call for an examination of the measurement, educational, and legal issues associated with teacher licensure testing. In its work thus far, the committee has focused on the measures used for initial licensure: those generally required for teachers before they enter the classroom. The committee acknowledges that some states have expanded their licensure systems to include assessments of teachers' performance. These measures will be examined in the committee's final report. The committee has begun to explore the current status of licensure testing and the literature on teacher licensure to assess what is known about existing systems. With limited time and resources, the committee was not able to conduct the extensive research that is needed to fully address many important questions about teaching and tests.

The committee's next report will examine the issues covered here in greater depth and may recommend model systems for licensing beginning teachers.

Current Licensure Testing

Licensure is a state function. It is aimed, above all, at protecting the public. As defined by the federal government, licensure is "the process by which an agency of government grants permission to persons to engage in a given profession or occupation by certifying that those licensed have attained the minimal degree of competency necessary to ensure that the public health, safety, and welfare will be reasonably well protected" (U.S. Department of Health, Education, and Welfare, 1971:7). States issue licenses for more than 900 professions, from lawyers and architects to food handlers and cosmetologists.

To be consistent with conventional parlance, this report uses the terms "licensure" and "licensure testing" to refer to the decisions that states make and the tools they use to make those decisions. However, this term is not precisely accurate when referring to teachers. Unlike members of other professions, teachers who do not earn licenses can teach in independent schools, and they can teach in public schools with temporary "emergency" permits or credentials.

Licensure is distinct from hiring. Although state licenses grant permission for teachers to teach in public schools, local agencies—school districts and, in many cases, schools—actually hire the teachers and so determine who will teach and what they will teach. The districts and schools that hire teachers may decide to use criteria in addition to the holding of a license in deciding which teachers to hire. They may also, depending on local needs, decide to hire teachers for positions for which they are not licensed. That is, schools may hire or place a teacher licensed to teach mathematics in science classes or one with a license to teach in middle schools in an elementary school.

VARIATION IN STATE POLICIES

In setting policies for licensing teachers, states determine the basic skills (usually reading, writing, and mathematics abilities), general knowledge, specific subject-matter knowledge, and knowledge about teaching and learning they believe beginning teachers ought to possess. States also establish the criteria for determining whether prospective teachers have these skills and knowledge. These criteria generally include coursework in state-approved teacher education programs at the undergraduate or graduate levels, a major or minor in the intended teaching field, and student-teaching experience. Forty-one states also require prospective teachers to pass one or more tests.

A growing number of states have supplemented college and university preparation programs for licensure with alternative routes for people to enter teaching from other fields. These routes often include an entrance requirement for content expertise and experience in the field. The candidates then participate in an intensive study of teaching and learning, and they are provided on-site supervision as beginning teachers. In most cases, such teachers are required to pass the same tests as those who become teachers through traditional routes.

Requirements vary widely across states. Approximately 30 states specify academic requirements for entry into a teacher preparation program. Nearly all states require prospective teachers to complete coursework—in content areas and pedagogy—in approved teacher-education programs. A few states, including Ohio, Connecticut, and Kansas, have abandoned prescriptive coursework requirements and have adopted instead broad-based standards or sets of competencies that must be mastered, presumably by completing a state's approved teacher preparation program.

Many states also include ancillary licensure requirements such as U.S. citizenship, minimum age, adequate health, good moral character, and allegiance to the government.

Eight states grant a permanent license for which there are no further requirements. The majority of states, though, have a two- or three-tiered licensure process. After earning a provisional license, which usually includes passing a test, teachers in these states typically must complete advanced degrees or continue professional development to earn a permanent license. A small number of states, including Ohio, North Carolina, and Connecticut, require demonstration of competent teaching practice to obtain the next level of license.

TYPES OF TESTS

The 41 states that require teachers to pass a test to earn a license vary widely in their practices. Tests are available to measure aspects of teacher knowledge, and state agencies have chosen different tests depending on what knowledge and skills they believe teachers ought to demonstrate. (See the appendix for a table showing the diversity of assessment requirements among state licensure systems.)

The content of the tests varies from the assessment of basic reading, writing, and mathematics skills to deep subject-matter knowledge to the demonstration of teaching skill. The format varies from multiple choice to constructed response. The tests assess five general aspects of teacher knowledge: basic skills, content knowledge, pedagogical knowledge, pedagogical content knowledge, and teaching performance.

Basic Skills. The most common type of test measures basic literacy and mathematics. Thirty-seven states assess prospective teachers' basic skills, using a variety of options. Twenty-four states have chosen Praxis I (formerly called the Pre-Professional Skills Test), the first part of the Praxis Series produced by the Educational Testing Service (ETS). According to ETS, Praxis I measures the basic knowledge in mathematics, reading, and writing deemed essential for all teachers.

The other 13 states have chosen to use basic skills tests specifically designed for their teacher-candidates. In five states, the basic skills test is designed by National Evaluation Systems (NES), with the test owned by the respective state (National Association of State Directors of Teacher Education and Certification, 1999). The remaining eight states have developed their own basic skills tests.

Subject-Matter Knowledge. In addition to the assessments of teachers' basic skills, 31 states require teachers to take a test on subject-matter knowledge. As with the basic skills tests, states can choose from among several options for this purpose. The Praxis II series (formerly the National Teacher Examinations) includes 140 such exams. The nine states that use tests designed for their states by NES also provide a range of subject-area tests. For example, New York offers 21 tests, and Michigan offers 78 tests. Florida has developed its own subject-matter knowledge tests.

Pedagogical Knowledge. Twenty-five states also use tests to assess teachers' pedagogical knowledge. Of these, 20 states use a component of Praxis II called the Principles of Learning and Teaching Tests. These tests are offered for prospective teachers in three grade levels: grades K-6, 5-9, and 7-12. The tests cover organizing content knowledge for student learning, creating an environment for student learning, teaching for student learning, and teacher professionalism. They are intended to draw on prospective teachers' knowledge of educational psychology, classroom management, instructional design and delivery techniques, and evaluation and assessment. NES has also developed pedagogical knowledge tests for a few states, including Oklahoma, Colorado, New York, and Texas. Florida has developed its own test of pedagogical knowledge, called the Florida Professional Education Test, and California has developed a professional knowledge test for reading instruction, called the Reading Instruction Competence Assessment.

Pedagogical Content Knowledge. There is another kind of teacher knowledge that includes dimensions of both subject-matter and pedagogical knowledge, termed pedagogical content knowledge. According to Shulman (1986:9), pedagogical content knowledge goes beyond the knowledge of subject matter to include the "dimension of subject-matter knowledge for teaching." This type of knowledge includes ways of formulating or representing subject matter to make it understandable to students, as well as an understanding of what makes learning a topic easy or difficult, for example, the misconceptions about the solar system that might impede a student's learning about astronomy.

The Praxis II series includes tests of pedagogical content knowledge in biology, foreign language, mathematics, physical education, physical science, social studies, and Spanish. However, few states require prospective teachers to take tests of pedagogical content knowledge.

Teaching Performance. In a handful of states, assessments of candidates' teaching performance is becoming part of the licensure system, so that beginning teachers must demonstrate competence in the classroom to qualify for a provisional teaching license. This interim report focuses on tests for initial licensure; the assessments of teaching performance will be considered in the final report.

WAIVERS TO LICENSING RULES

While the licensure rules and test requirements generally determine who is eligible to teach in public schools, two-thirds of the states allow waivers of the rules to allow districts to hire teachers on an emergency basis if they cannot find enough licensed teachers in particular fields. Some states allow the hiring of teachers with no license; other states issue emergency or temporary licenses to individuals who have met some requirements (such as a bachelor's degree, passage of a basic skills test, or a license from another state), but who have not fulfilled all the licensure requirements.

In all but three states that require basic-skills tests, the test requirements may be waived or delayed for emergency licenses; subject-matter test requirements may be waived in all but one state (New Jersey) that require them. In some cases, these waiver policies may mean that districts can hire teachers who have failed licensure tests (*Education Week*, 2000).

The number of teachers employed with emergency permits or credentials varies widely across states, and state rules differ as to which licensure requirements may be waived for teachers using emergency credentials. The number of teachers with emergency licenses is substantial in some states, particularly in some districts or fields within states. For example, in Texas, 42,470 teachers

(17.6 percent of the state's teaching force) received waivers from licensure requirements in 1996-1997; 22.6 percent (4,012 of 17,759) of mathematics teachers in Texas that year were teaching with waivers. In some states, however, the number of teachers with waivers is relatively small: in Washington State, 418 of the state's 62,607 teachers (0.7 percent) held waivers in 1998 (U.S. Department of Education, 1999).

The proportion of teachers with waivers tends to be higher in high-poverty districts than in low-poverty districts. For example, in Maryland in 1999, 2 percent of teachers in low-poverty districts (425 of 20,813) had waivers, compared with 8.5 percent (2,351 of 27,676) in high-poverty districts (U.S. Department of Education, 1999).

TEST USE AND PASSING SCORES

In addition to using different types of tests, states also use tests in different ways. For example, some states require basic skills tests for admittance into teacher education programs, while other states require candidates to take such tests after completing such programs.

Each state also establishes its own passing scores for the tests it requires. These scores vary widely even when states use the same test. As an example, consider the minimum scores different states require on the Praxis subject-matter tests (see Figure 1). The range of passing scores on Praxis II Mathematics: Content Knowledge goes from 124 to 147 (of possible scores of 100-200). In 1997-1998, the lowest passing score set by states (124) placed candidates slightly above the 20th percentile in the national distribution of all takers, while the highest passing score set (147) was at about the 75th percentile.

It is virtually impossible to make meaningful comparisons of passing scores across states when states use their own tests. The variations in the content and format of the tests, the average difficulty of their questions, the different times (in candidates' teacher education programs) at which they are administered, and the way the results are reported and used to make pass/fail decisions pose substantial obstacles to making valid comparisons of scores and passing rates across states (National Research Council, 1998).

COMPARISONS OF PASSING RATES

Title II of the Higher Education Act of 1998 requires reports by states and institutions of higher education of passing rates on licensure tests. A preliminary report, released in December 1999, uses data provided by the states to show the testing requirements for each state and the passing rate for each institution within the state (U.S. Department of Education, 1999). In the future, the Secretary of Education is required to produce a national "report card" that includes the passing rates in each state and each institution within the state, along with information on

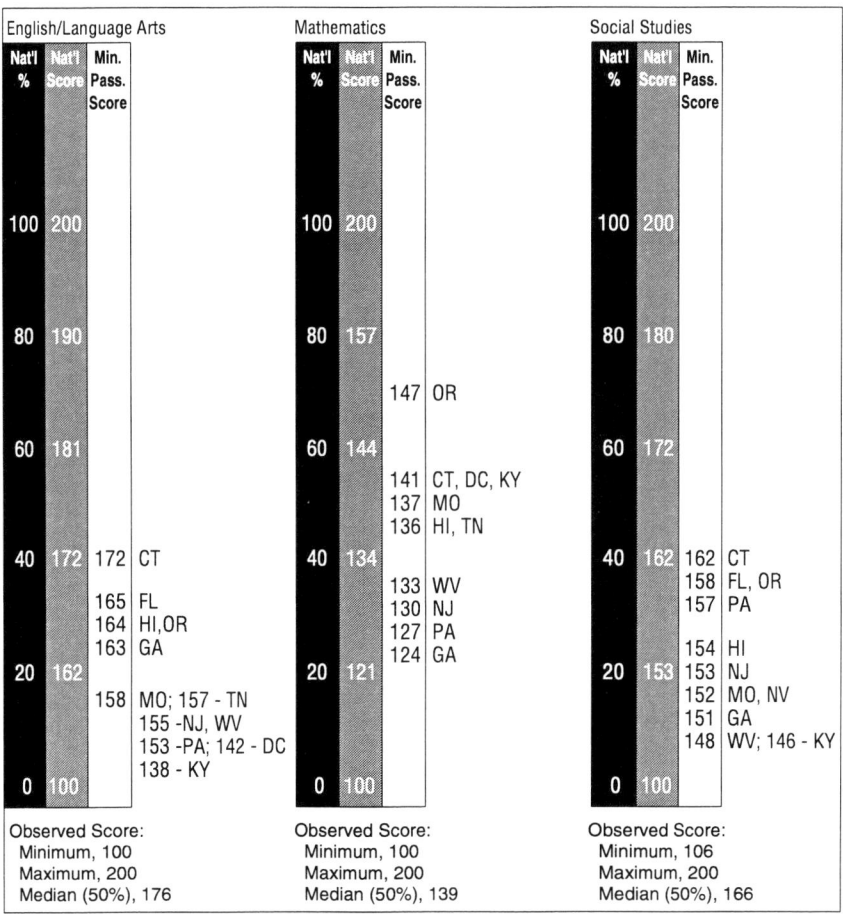

FIGURE 1 State minimum passing scores on the ETS Praxis Content area tests, by score percentile: 1997-1998. SOURCE: U.S. Department of Education (1999: Graph 2).

the state's efforts to improve teacher quality. The report is also expected to include the national mean and median scores on licensure tests used in more than one state. The forthcoming reports are expected to rely on a common set of definitions, currently being developed by the National Center for Education Statistics, that will help ensure that the states and institutions mean the same thing when they indicate who belongs in the pool of test takers and the pool of those who passed.

However, the variability in tests, passing scores, and student populations across states makes meaningful comparisons of passing rates extremely difficult.

What does it mean if State A, which requires graduates to pass Praxis I to earn a license, has a passing rate of 80 percent, while State B, which uses a different test, has a passing rate of 55 percent?

The law also requires institutions to include data on passing rates in school catalogues and materials provided to high school counselors. The legislation further allows states to consider many factors in determining when an institution is "low performing." Thus, the law recognizes that passing rates may vary among institutions of higher education as a result of differences in their policies and the characteristics of their students, as well as in the quality of the instruction they provide.

Unfortunately, the public may not have enough specific information about each institution to make valid comparisons in passing rates among them. For example, institutions that restrict entry to teacher education programs are likely to have higher passing rates than those that are less restrictive and whose mission is focused on providing opportunity for all students. Institutions also have different policies for testing: some administer tests upon entry to teacher education programs; others administer them at the conclusion of the program and provide multiple opportunities for candidates to pass the tests. Such policies are likely to affect passing rates even though they may have little or nothing to do with the quality of the institution's educational programs.

The Development and Quality of Licensure Tests

The *Standards for Educational and Psychological Testing* (American Educational Research Association et al., 1985, 1999), the *Principles for the Validation and Use of Personnel Selection Procedures: Third Edition* (Society for Industrial and Organizational Psychology, 1987), and the *Uniform Guidelines for Employee Selection Procedures* (U.S. Equal Employment Opportunity Commission et al., 29 C.F.R. 1607, 1978 ed.), provide guidelines for developing educational, psychological, and employment tests and for gathering validity evidence about their uses. They outline criteria for evaluating tests and testing practices.

TEST DEVELOPMENT

As noted above, licensure tests are designed to distinguish between candidates who meet minimum professional standards and those who do not. Developers of basic skills and content knowledge tests often begin the design process by conducting analyses to determine the knowledge and skills that beginning teachers need to demonstrate before they should be allowed to practice without direct supervision (Pearlman, 1999). These analyses rely on data that ranges from informed judgments to formal surveys.

For basic skills tests, rudimentary literacy and mathematics skills are identified. For subject-matter and pedagogical knowledge tests, the analyses draw on national disciplinary standards, such as the mathematics standards developed by the National Council of Teachers of Mathematics (National Council of Teachers of Mathematics, 1989) and science education standards developed by the National Research Council (National Research Council, 1996); state standards for students and teachers; and the research literature. For some subject-matter and pedagogical knowledge tests, the knowledge and skill listings go out for public review and comment before test content is defined; in others, developers survey teachers to determine which of these competencies are important (Porter et al., in press). Using this information, test developers then construct test specifications that describe the content of teacher licensure tests and the ways the content will be assessed. Though there are commonalties, test specifications differ from state to state in accordance with state judgments about the knowledge and skills needed for beginning teachers.

Test developers, often with the assistance of practitioners, write questions that meet the specifications. These questions typically are then reviewed for accuracy, clarity, and fairness. In many cases, field trials of questions are conducted before the final tests are constructed.

Once test are built, developers and state licensing officials set passing standards on them. Generally, teachers are asked to estimate the level of performance on the test minimally qualified candidates would be expected to achieve. Often, panels of educators are asked to judge whether adequately prepared beginning teachers would answer particular questions correctly; these question-by-question judgments are compiled to derive a recommended overall passing score. Alternatively, teachers examine entire test booklets to estimate the lowest score a candidate could earn and still be considered minimally qualified.

The final determination of passing scores usually is made by each state's board of education, based on the panels' recommendations and other information, such as the estimated effect of different passing scores on passing rates and the number of licensed teachers. As noted above, even when the same test is used, passing scores vary by state, depending, in part, on differing views of minimum standards for teachers.

The test development and standard-setting procedures described here are generally consistent with professional guidelines and are used by the Educational Testing Service and several state licensing agencies. Other developers and states have taken different approaches to constructing teacher licensure tests and setting passing scores. In addition, there are differences in the composition and backgrounds of question writers and reviewers, and in the makeup of standard-setting panels. For some tests, public documentation is insufficient to judge the quality of test development efforts. Some tests have been criticized for failing to adhere to professional test development guidelines, but the committee has not reviewed the validity of these criticisms.

VALIDITY EVIDENCE

In addition to providing information on test development procedures, test developers are also expected to provide evidence of the validity of test score interpretation. Most of the validity evidence currently available for teacher licensure tests is based on judgments about whether the test is likely to assess the knowledge and skills it was intended to measure and whether such knowledge and skills are necessary for beginning teachers to possess (Educational Testing Service, 1999; Mehrens, 1990; Popham, 1990). For basic skills tests, this evidence is based on judgments about the literacy and mathematics abilities beginning teachers should demonstrate. That is, state panels describe the reading, writing, and mathematics skills all teachers should have, and they judge whether the tests are likely to measure such knowledge. For subject-matter and pedagogical tests, the validity evidence rests on judgments about what beginning teachers should know about curriculum and instruction and whether given test items cover that information.

Developers and state sponsors often collect this evidence by convening panels of educators to make judgments about whether the knowledge and skills the items appear to measure match the test specifications and whether the knowledge is important for entry-level teachers to demonstrate. In some states these data are collected as part of the test adoption process.

These judgments about the importance of the knowledge and skills tested (and the appropriateness of passing scores) are used as indicators of test quality. Validity evidence based on test content helps provide assurance to policy makers, teacher candidates, and the public that the test measures what it purports to measure and that test results indicate the extent to which teachers are likely to possess the knowledge and skills considered necessary for teaching. Such evidence also has been used to uphold teacher licensure tests in at least two legal challenges (*Association of Mexican American Educators v. California*, 183 F.3d 1055, 1070-1071, 9th Cir., 1999; *United States v. South Carolina*, 445 F. Supp. 1094, D. S.C., 1977). Similarly, evidence that test developers did not follow professional standards has been used to bar the use of teacher tests (*Richardson v. Lamar County Board of Education et al.*, 729 F Supp. 806, 820-21, M.D. Ala., 1989, aff'd 935 F 2d 1240, 5th Cir.).

It is important to note that the tests used for initial licensure—basic skills, subject-matter knowledge, and pedagogical knowledge—are not designed to measure effective teaching. Effective teaching requires many skills and types of knowledge. A given test that is used in the teacher licensing process may measure only some of these. Thus, passing such a test will not insure that a teacher will be effective in the classroom. For example, a state may determine that all teachers must be able to read at a particular level, or that all teachers must know some basic mathematics, regardless of whether their reading and computing skills are correlated with their overall effectiveness as a teacher. While this information may be deemed necessary, it is not sufficient for determining whether a candidate will be a successful teacher.

Currently, there is little research to show the relationship between candidates' scores on teacher licensing tests and their performance in the classroom. In part, the data are scant because it is methodologically difficult to investigate these relationships. Some of the many obstacles include the difficulty of measuring teachers' effectiveness in the classroom and the lack of a commonly accepted valid and fair measure of effective teaching. In addition, the research is hampered by the difficulty in accurately distinguishing minimally competent from minimally incompetent classroom practice, the absence of job performance information for some unlicensed examinees, and the fact that some good teaching practice is context-specific—that is, it varies by student population, educational goals, school organization, community characteristics, and other factors.

Although it is difficult to examine the relationship between scores on teacher licensure tests and job performance, it is certainly possible and important to study these. Analyses of the relationship between scores on teacher licensure tests and effectiveness in the classroom would provide useful evidence about the validity of teacher licensure tests and could provide a better understanding of what the tests do and do not measure.

Several current test development efforts respond to the limits of the evidentiary base about and possible limitations in past and current teacher tests. One such effort is the work of the Interstate New Teacher Assessment and Support Consortium (INTASC), a group of 32 states that are developing standards for beginning teachers and related assessments. In part, INTASC's work is directed at establishing a broad consensus on knowledge and skill standards for beginning teachers and at achieving a better representation and measurement of those important teacher competencies (Porter et al., 2000).

Even under the best of circumstances, tests cannot be expected to measure everything that is important for success in the classroom, just as licensure tests in medicine and law do not measure all the qualities required for success in those professions. Teaching quality depends on many things. Obviously, teachers must be knowledgeable and know how to teach, but good teachers can explain ideas so that different students understand them; they are also compassionate, resourceful, committed, honest, and persistent in their efforts to help children learn. All of these things are important to teaching but difficult to measure. A single test or set of tests can only measure some of the characteristics associated with competent teaching. Nevertheless, this difficulty does not negate the value of assessing basic skills, subject-matter knowledge, and pedagogical knowledge.

Disparate Impact

As with many licensure tests in other professions, white candidates pass teacher licensure tests at higher rates than black and Hispanic candidates. With repeated retaking, black and Hispanic candidates' pass rates approach those of whites, but the differences are still substantial, and it is not certain how many candidates drop out of the pool after failing the test the first time. Nevertheless, the gap in eventual pass rates has contributed to practical problems for schools that want to hire a diverse teaching force, and it has led to legal challenges.

What is the performance gap? Although comprehensive national data are not available, results from Praxis provide some indication of its extent. From 1994-1997, 87 percent of whites, compared with 53 percent of African Americans and 77 percent of Hispanics, passed the Praxis I examination of basic skills. On the Praxis II tests of content and pedagogical knowledge, 92 percent of whites passed during the 3-year period, compared with 65 percent of African Americans and 46 percent of Hispanics (Gitomer et al., 1999). In this study, the researchers examined only the last test taken by examinees in the 3-year period. Thus, the proportion of candidates who passed may include those who failed initially and passed on a subsequent try; the failure rate may include those who passed after 1997.

Differential pass rates, in and of themselves, do not signify that teacher licensure tests are biased or otherwise unfair. But because of the differences in passing rates, licensure tests have been challenged in court on civil rights grounds. Under Title VII of the Civil Rights Act of 1964, employers are prohibited from using employment practices that discriminate on the basis of race, sex, or national origin.

Two appeals courts have ruled that Title VII does not apply to teacher licensure tests, because minimum standards for the profession are not employment standards. In *Fields v. Hallsville Independent School District* (906 F. 2nd 1017, 5th Cir., 1990), the U.S. Court of Appeals for the Fifth Circuit simply described the teacher-certification test as a licensure test. In a more recent case, the U.S. Circuit Court of Appeals for the Ninth Circuit, ruling in a case involving the use of the California Basic Educational Skills Test, ruled that Title VII does not apply in part because school districts, not the state, were the employers of teachers. The court also ruled that the test was not biased and that no valid alternative, with less of a disparate impact, was available (*Association of Mexican American Educators v. California*, 183 F.3d 1055, 1070-1071, 9th Cir., 1999).

A federal district court in South Carolina, however, relied on the standards of Title VII in its ruling on a teacher licensure test in that state. The court ruled that, despite a disparate impact on black applicants, the state was justified in using the test (the National Teacher Examinations) (*United States v. South Carolina*, 445 F. Supp. 1094, D. S.C., 1977). The U.S. Supreme Court summarily affirmed the lower court's ruling, in its only ruling on teacher licensure tests (*National Education Association v. South Carolina*, 434 U.S. 1026, 1978).

The problem of disparate impact is not unique to teacher licensure tests. Indeed, other licensing tests, such as bar examinations, show similar gaps in passing rates (Klein and Bolus, 1997). However, the racial and ethnic disparities create particular problems in education, since many schools seek a teaching staff that is racially and ethnically diverse, particularly if they serve a large proportion of minority students. Although there are many factors that limit schools' ability to achieve this goal, the disparities in passing rates contribute to the difficulty schools face in attracting a diverse teaching staff. Evidence of the validity of test score information and the appropriateness of passing scores are needed to determine whether many blacks and Hispanics are screened out from public-school teaching inappropriately.

Conclusions

As a result of its preliminary explorations and discussions, the Committee on Assessment and Teacher Quality has reached five conclusions:

- Licensure tests are designed to provide useful information about the extent to which prospective teachers possess the literacy and mathematics skills and/or the subject-matter and pedagogical knowledge that states consider necessary for beginning teaching.
- Teacher licensure tests assess only some of the characteristics that are deemed to be important for effective practice. They are not designed to predict who will become effective teachers.
- There is currently little evidence available about the extent to which widely used teacher licensure tests distinguish between candidates who are minimally competent to teach and those who are not.
- Comparisons of passing rates among states are not useful for policy purposes because of the diversity of testing and licensure practices.
- Test instruments, pass/fail rules, and other licensing requirements and policies that result in large differences in eventual passing rates among racial/ethnic groups pose problems for schools that seek to have a diverse teaching force.

Appendix

Summary of Assessments Offered for Initial Teacher Certification and Licensure, by State: 1998

State	Data not obtained	No assessments required	Number of written tests offered*	Written Tests			
				Basic Skills	Professional Knowledge of Teaching		
					Elementary	Middle Grades	Secondary
Alabama		X	NA	NA	NA	NA	NA
Alaska			6	Yes	No	No	No
Arizona			32	Yes	Yes—same test	Yes—same test	Yes—same test
Arkansas			51	Yes	Yes	Yes	Yes
California			51	Yes	Yes—same test	Yes—same test	Yes—same test
Colorado			41	Yes	Yes	Yes	Yes
Connecticut			42	Yes	No	Yes	No
Delaware			11	Yes	No	No	No
District of Columbia			30	Yes	No	No	No
Florida			66	Yes	Yes—same test	Yes—same test	Yes—same test
Georgia			51	Yes	No	Yes	No
Hawaii			42	Yes	Yes	Yes	Yes
Idaho		X	NA	NA	NA	NA	NA
Illinois			45	Yes	Yes	Yes	Yes
Indiana			35	Yes	Yes—same test	Yes—same test	Yes—same test
Iowa		X	NA	NA	NA	NA	NA
Kansas			4	Yes	Yes—same test	Yes—same test	Yes—same test
Kentucky			50	Yes	Yes—same test	Yes—same test	Yes—same test
Louisiana			26	Yes	Yes	Yes	Yes
Maine			8	Yes	No	No	No
Maryland			42	Yes	No	Yes	Yes
Massachusetts			44	Yes	No	No	No
Michigan			75	Yes	No	No	No
Minnesota			6	Yes	No	No	No

Subject	Written Tests			Performance Tests	
	Other			Portfolios Observation	Classroom
	Special Ed.	Early Ch. Ed.	Reading		
NA	NA	NA	NA	NA	NA
No	No	No	No	No	No
Yes	Yes	Yes	No	No	No
Yes	Yes	Yes	No	No	No
Yes	No	No	Yes	No	No
Yes	Yes	Yes	Yes	No	No
Yes	Yes	No	No	Yes	Yes
No	No	No	No	No	No
Yes	Yes	Yes	No	No	No
Yes	Yes	Yes	No	No	No
Yes	Yes	Yes	Yes	No	No
Yes	Yes	No	No	No	No
NA	NA	NA	NA	NA	NA
Yes	Yes	Yes	Yes	No	No
Yes	Yes	Yes	Yes	No	No
NA	NA	NA	NA	NA	NA
No	No	No	No	No	No
Yes	Yes	No	No	No	No
Yes	No	Yes	No	No	No
No	No	No	No	No	No
Yes	Yes	Yes	No	No	No
Yes	Yes	Yes	Yes	No	No
Yes	Yes	Yes	Yes	No	No
No	No	No	No	No	No

State	Data not obtained	No assessments required	Number of written tests offered*	Written Tests			
				Basic Skills	Professional Knowledge of Teaching		
					Elementary	Middle Grades	Secondary
Mississippi			36	Yes	Yes	Yes	Yes
Missouri			32	Yes	No	Yes	Yes
Montana			6	Yes	No	No	No
Nebraska			7	Yes	No	No	No
Nevada			47	Yes	Yes	Yes	Yes
New Hampshire			6	Yes	No	No	No
New Jersey			21	No	No	No	No
New Mexico			6	Yes	Yes–same test	Yes–same test	Yes–same test
New York			28	Yes	Yes	No	Yes
North Carolina			57	Yes	Yes	Yes	Yes
North Dakota		X	NA	NA	NA	NA	NA
Ohio			39	No	Yes	Yes	Yes
Oklahoma			42	Yes	Yes	Yes	Yes
Oregon			64	Yes	Yes–same test	Yes–same test	Yes–same test
Pennsylvania			45	Yes	Yes	Yes	Yes
Rhode Island			3	Yes	Yes–same test	Yes–same test	Yes–same test
South Carolina			29	No	Yes	Yes	Yes
South Dakota		X	NA	NA	NA	NA	NA
Tennessee			65	Yes	Yes	Yes	Yes
Texas			60	No	Yes	No	Yes
Utah		X	NA	NA	NA	NA	NA
Vermont		X	NA	NA	NA	NA	NA
Virginia			32	Yes	No	No	No
Washington		X	NA	NA	NA	NA	NA

				Performance Tests	
Subject	Other			Portfolios Observation	Classroom
	Special Ed.	Early Ch. Ed.	Reading		
Yes	Yes	No	No	No	No
Yes	Yes	Yes	No	No	No
No	No	No	No	No	No
No	No	No	No	No	No
Yes	Yes	No	Yes	No	No
No	No	No	No	No	No
Yes	No	No	Yes	No	No
No	No	No	No	No	No
Yes	No	Yes	No	No	No
Yes	Yes	No	Yes	No	No
NA	NA	NA	NA	NA	NA
Yes	Yes	Yes	Yes	Yes	Yes
Yes	Yes	Yes	No	No	No
Yes	Yes	Yes	No	No	No
Yes	Yes	Yes	Yes	No	No
No	No	No	No	No	No
Yes	Yes	Yes	Yes	No	No
NA	NA	NA	NA	NA	NA
Yes	Yes	Yes	No	No	No
Yes	Yes	Yes	Yes	No	No
NA	NA	NA	NA	NA	NA
NA	NA	NA	NA	NA	NA
Yes	Yes	Yes	No	No	No
NA	NA	NA	NA	NA	NA

					Written Tests		
State	Data not obtained	No assessments required	Number of written tests offered*	Basic Skills	Professional Knowledge of Teaching		
					Elementary	Middle Grades	Secondary
West Virginia			49	Yes	Yes	Yes	Yes
Wisconsin			6	Yes	No	No	No
Wyoming		X	NA	NA	NA	NA	NA
American Samoa	X		not obtained	not obtained	not obtained	not obtained	not obtained
Department of Defense Education Activity			7	Yes	Yes–same test	Yes–same test	Yes–same test
Federated States of Micronesia	X		not obtained	not obtained	not obtained	not obtained	not obtained
Guam			1	Yes	No	No	No
Northern Mariana Islands		X	NA	NA	NA	NA	NA
Puerto Rico			2	Yes	Yes–same test	Yes–same test	Yes–same test
Virgin Islands	X		not obtained	not obtained	not obtained	not obtained	not obtained

*The number of tests offered as reported by the state. All offered tests are not taken every year.

NA = Not Applicable

SOURCE: U.S. Department of Education (1999:Table B).

INTERIM REPORT

				Performance Tests	
Subject	Other			Portfolios Observation	Classroom
	Special Ed.	Early Ch. Ed.	Reading		
Yes	Yes	Yes	Yes	No	No
No	No	No	No	No	No
NA	NA	NA	NA	NA	NA
not obtained	not obtained	not obtained	not obtained	not obtained	not obtained
No	No	No	No	No	No
not obtained	not obtained	not obtained	not obtained	not obtained	not obtained
No	No	No	No	No	No
NA	NA	NA	NA	NA	NA
No	No	No	No	No	No
not obtained	not obtained	not obtained	not obtained	not obtained	not obtained

References

American Educational Research Association, American Psychological Association, and National Council on Measurement in Education
    1985   *Standards for Educational and Psychological Testing*. Washington, DC: American Psychological Association.
    1999   *Standards for Educational and Psychological Testing*. Washington, DC: American Educational Research Association.

Darling-Hammond, L., A. E. Wise, and S. P. Klein
    1999   *A License to Teach*. San Francisco, CA: Westview Press, Inc.

Education Week
    2000   Quality Counts 2000: Who should teach? *Education Week* 19 (Jan. 31).

Educational Testing Service
    1999   *Understanding Teacher Assessment: Validity for Licensing Tests*. Teaching and Learning Division. Princeton, NJ.

Gitomer, Drew H., Andrew S. Latham, and Robert Ziomek
    1999   *The Academic Quality of Prospective Teachers: The Impact of Admissions and Licensure Testing*. Princeton, NJ: Educational Testing Service.

Haertel, Edward H.
    1991   New forms of teacher assessment. In *Review of Research in Education*, Gerald Grant, ed. Volume 17. Washington, DC: American Educational Research Association.

Haney, Walter M., George Madaus, and Amelia Kreitzer
    1987   Charms talismanic: Testing teachers for the improvement of education. In *Review of Research in Education, Volume 14*. Ernst Z. Rothkopf, ed. Washington, DC: American Educational Research Association.

Klein, S., and R. Bolus
    1997   The size and source of differences in bar exam passing rates among racial and ethnic groups. *The Bar Examiner* 66: 8-16.

Mehrens, William A.
   1990 Assessing the quality of teacher assessment tests. In *Assessment of Teaching: Purposes, Practices, and Implications for the Profession.* James V. Mitchell, Steven L. Wise, and Barbara S. Plake, eds. Hillsdale, NJ: Lawrence M. Erlbaum Associates, Publishers.

National Association of State Directors of Teacher Education and Certification
   1999 *The NASDTEC Manual 1998-1999: Manual on the Preparation and Certification of Educational Personnel.* Theodore Andrews and Laura Andrews, eds. Dubuque, IA: Kendall/Hunt Publishing Company.

National Commission on Teaching and America's Future
   1996 *What Matters Most: Teaching for America's Future.* Report of the National Commission on Teaching & America's Future. September 1996. New York: Teachers College, Columbia University.

National Council of Teachers of Mathematics
   1989 *Curriculum and Evaluation Standards for School Mathematics.* Reston, VA: National Council of Teachers of Mathematics.

National Research Council
   1996 *National Science Education Standards.* National Committee on Science Education Standards and Assessment, Center for Science, Mathematics, and Engineering Education. Washington, DC: National Academy Press.
   1998 *Uncommon Measures: Equivalence and Linking Among Educational Tests.* Committee on Equivalency and Linkage of Educational Tests. Michael J. Feuer, Paul W. Holland, Bert F. Green, Meryl W. Bertenthal, and F. Cadelle Hemphill, eds. Board on Testing and Assessment. Washington, DC: National Academy Press.

Pearlman, Mari
   1999 K-12 Math and Science Education—Testing and Licensing Teachers. Testimony of Educational Testing Service before the House Science Committee, August 4. Educational Testing Service, Princeton, NJ.

Popham, W. James
   1990 Face validity: siren song for teacher tests. In *Assessment of Teaching: Purposes, Practices, and Implications for the Profession.* James V. Mitchell, Steven L. Wise, and Barbara S. Plake, eds. Hillsdale, NJ: Lawrence M. Erlbaum Associates, Publishers.

Porter, Andrew C., Peter Youngs, and Allan Odden
   2000 Advances in teacher assessments and their uses. In *Handbook of Research on Teaching.* Fourth edition. V. Richardson, ed. Washington, DC: American Educational Research Association.

Society for Industrial and Organizational Psychology
   1987 *Principles for the Validation and Use of Personnel Selection Procedures.* Third Edition. College Park, MD: Society for Industrial and Organizational Psychology.

Shulman, Lee
   1986 Those who understand: Knowledge growth in teaching. *Educational Researcher* 15(2): 4-14.

U.S. Department of Education
   1999 *The Initial Report of the Secretary on the Quality of Teacher Preparation.* Washington, DC: Office of Postsecondary Education, U.S. Department of Education.

U.S. Department of Health, Education and Welfare
   1971 *Report on licensure and related health personnel credentialing.* PHEW Publication 72-11. Washington, DC: U.S. Department of Health, Education and Welfare.

Bibliography

American Council on Education
    1999 *To Touch the Future: Transforming the Way Teachers are Taught: An Action Agenda for College and University Professors.* American Washington, DC: Council on Education Fulfillment Service.

American Federation of Teachers
    1999 *Teaching Reading Is Rocket Science: What Expert Teachers of Reading Should Know and Be Able To Do.* Washington, DC: American Federation of Teachers.

Archer, Jeff
    1998 States raising bar for teachers despite pending shortage. *Education Week* (March 25).

Association of Mexican American Educators v. California, 183 F.3d 1055, 1070-1071 (9th Cir., 1999).

Ayers, J.B., and G.S. Qualls
    1979 Concurrent and predictive validity of the National Teacher Examinations. *Journal of Educational Research* 72 (2):86-92.

Ballou, Dale, and Michael Podgorsky
    1997 *Reforming teacher training and recruitment: A critical appraisal of the recommendations of the National Commission on Teaching and America's Future.* Government Union Review *17(4).* Available: http://www.psrf.org/doc/v74_art.html (3/21/2000).

Berk, Ronald A.
    1990 Limitations on using student-achievement data for career-ladder promotions and merit-pay decisions. In *Assessment of Teaching: Purposes, Practices, and Implications for the Profession*, James V. Mitchell, Steven L. Wise, and Barbara S. Plake, eds. Hillsdale, NJ: Lawrence M. Erlbaum Associates, Publishers.

Berliner, David
    1984 Remarks to the Governor's Task Force on Teacher Education (February 16). University of Arizona, Tucson.

Bruschi, Barbara, and Richard J. Coley
    1999 *How Teachers Compare: The Prose, Document, and Quantitative Skills of America's Teachers.* Princeton, NJ: Policy Information Center, Educational Testing Service.

Cohen, David K., and Heather Hill
  1998 *Instructional Policy and Classroom Performance: The Mathematics Reform in California.* Ann Arbor: University of Michigan.
Crocker, Linda
  1999 Evaluating Teacher Licensure Assessment Programs: Do the Old Criteria Apply to Emergent Assessments? Paper prepared for the Committee on Assessment and Teacher Quality (September). University of Florida, Gainesville.
Darling-Hammond, L., A.E. Wise, and S.P. Klein
  1999 *A License to Teach.* San Francisco, CA: Westview Press, Inc.
Educational Testing Service
  1999 *Understanding Teacher Assessment: Significant Decisions in Testing Litigation.* Princeton, NJ: Teaching and Learning Division.
  1999 *Understanding Teacher Assessment: Setting Passing Scores: The Need for Justifiable Procedures.* Princeton, NJ: Teaching and Learning Division.
  1998 *The Use of Praxis Pass Rates to Evaluate Teacher Education Programs: An ETS Background Report.* Washington, DC: State and Federal Relations Office, Educational Testing Service.
  1997 *Validation and Standard-Setting Procedures Used for Tests in the Praxis Series.* Princeton, NJ: Educational Testing Service.
Ellet, C.D., W. Capie, and C.E. Johnson
  1981 *Teacher Performance And Elementary Pupil Achievement on the Georgia Criterion Referenced Tests.* Athens: Teacher Assessment Project, University of Georgia.
Elmore, Richard F.
  1997 *Investing in Teacher Learning: Staff Development and Instructional Improvement in Community District #2, New York City.* New York: National Commission on Teaching and America's Future.
Equal Employment Opportunity Commission, Civil Service Commission, Department of Labor and Department of Justice
  1978 Uniform guidelines on employee selection procedures. *Federal Register* 43:38290-38315 (August 25).
Ferguson, Ronald F.
  1998 Can schools narrow the black-white test score gap? In *The Black-White Test Score Gap*, Christopher Jencks and Meredith Phillips, eds. Harrisonburg, VA: Brookings Institute.
  1998 Teachers' perceptions and expectations and the black-white test score gap. In *The Black-White Test Score Gap*, Christopher Jencks and Meredith Phillips, eds. Harrisonburg, VA: Brookings Institute.
Fields v. Hallsville Independent School District, 906 F. 2nd 1017 (5th Cir., 1990).
Fitzgerald, Kathleen J., and Peter M. Hall
  1999 Process, Perspectives, and Politics: Restructuring and Undergraduate Teacher Education Program. Paper presented at the AERA Conference, Montreal, Canada (April). University of Missouri, Columbia, MO.
Gitomer, Drew H., and Mari A. Pearlman
  1999 Are Teacher Licensing Tests Too Easy? Are Standards Too Low? A Response to the Education Trust. Paper prepared for the Committee on Assessment and Teacher Quality (September). Educational Testing Service, Princeton, NJ.
Goldhaber, Dan D.
  1999 Criteria of an Effective Teacher Licensure System. Paper prepared for the National Research Council for the Committee on Assessment and Teacher Quality (September). Urban Institute, Washington, DC.

Goldhaber, Dan D., and Dominic J. Brewer
  1998 Does Teacher Certification Matter? High School Certification Status and Student Achievement. Paper submitted to *Educational Evaluation and Policy Analysis*. Urban Institute, Washington, DC.
Haertel, Edward H.
  1991 New forms of teacher assessment. In *Review of Research in Education*, Volume 17, Gerald Grant, ed. Washington, DC: American Educational Research Association.
Haney, Walt, Clarke Fowler, Anne Wheelock, Damian Bebell and Nicole Malec
  1999 Less truth than error? An independent study of the Massachusetts Teacher Tests. *Educational Policy Analysis Archives* 7(4)(February 11). Available: http://epaa.asu.edu/epaa/v4/ (3/22/2000).
Haselkorn, David, and Louis Harris
  1997 *The Essential Profession: A National Survey of Public Attitudes Toward Teaching, Educational Opportunity and School Reform*. Belmont, MA: Recruiting New Teachers, Inc.
Haycock, Katie
  1998 Good teaching matters ... a lot. In *Thinking K-16* 3(2):1-14.
Hussar, William J.
  1998 *Predicting the Need for Newly Hired Teachers in the United States to 2008-09*. Washington, DC: National Center for Education Statistics, U.S. Department of Education.
Ingersoll, Richard M.
  1999 The problem of underqualified teacher in american secondary schools. *Educational Researcher* 28(2):26-37.
Jaeger, Richard
  1999 Some Psychometric Criteria for Judging the Quality of Teacher Certification Tests. Paper prepared for the Committee on Assessment and Teacher Quality (September). University of North Carolina, Greensboro.
Kennedy, Mary
  1992 The problem of improving teacher quality while balancing supply and demand. In *Teacher Supply, Demand, and Quality: Policy Issues, Models and Data Bases*. Erling Boe and Dorothy Gilford, eds. Committee on National Statistics and Division of Education, Training and Employment, Commission on Behavioral and Social Sciences, National Research Council. Washington, DC: National Academy Press.
Kirby, Sheila, Nataraj, Mark Berends, and Scott Haftel
  1999 Supply and demand of minority teachers in Texas: Problems and prospects. *Educational Evaluation and Policy Analysis* 21(1):47-66.
Klein, Stephen P.
  1998 Standards for teacher tests. *Journal of Personnel Evaluation in Education* 12(2):123-138.
Klein, Stephen P., and Brian Stecher
  1991 Developing a Prototype Licensing Examination for Secondary School Teachers. *Journal of Personnel Evaluation in Education* 5:169-190.
Klein, S., and R. Bolus
  1996 The size and source of differences in bar exam passing rates among racial and ethnic groups. *The Bar Examiner* 66: 8-16.
Lewis, Laurie, Basmat Parsad, Nancy Carey, Nicole Bartfai, Elizabeth Farris, and Becky Smerdon
  1999 Teacher Quality: A Report on the Preparation and Qualifications of Public School Teachers. *Education Statistics Quaterly* 1(1):7-14.
Livingston, Samuel A., and Michael J. Zieky
  1982 *Passing Scores: A Manual for Setting Standards of Performance on Educational and Occupational Tests*. Princeton, NJ: Educational Testing Service.

Medley, D.M., and T.J. Quirk
  1974 The application of a factorial design to the study of cultural bias in general culture items on the National Teacher Examination. *Journal of Educational Measurement* 11(4):235-245.

Melnick, S., and Diana Pullin
  1987 Teacher certification tests: Do they really measure what we need to know? *Phi Delta Kappan* (September):31-38.

Mezzacappa, Dale
  1998 Amendment seeks to teach a lesson to colleges of education. *Philadelphia Inquirer* April 29.

Mitchell, Ruth, and Patte Barth
  1999 How teacher licensing tests fall short. In *Thinking K-16* (Spring):1-23.

Moss, Pamela
  1998 Rethinking validity in the assessment of teaching. *With Portfolio in Hand: Portfolios in Teaching and Teacher Education*, N. Lyons and G. Grant, eds. New York: Teachers College Press.

Moss, Pamela, Aaron Schutz, and Kathleen M. Collins
  1998 An integrative approach to portfolio evaluation for teacher licensure. *Journal of Personnel Evaluation in Education* 12(2):139-161.

National Center for Education Statistics
  1999 *Teacher Quality: A Report on the Preparation and Qualification of Public School Teachers.* Statistical Analysis Report, January. Washington, DC: Office of Educational Research and Improvement, U.S. Department of Education.

National Research Council
  1998 *Myths and Tradeoffs: The Role of Tests in Undergraduate Admissions.* Steering Committee for the Workshop on Higher Education Admissions, Board on Testing and Assessment and Office of Scientific and Engineering Personnel, National Research Council. Washington, DC: National Academy Press.

Nweke, Winifred C., and Thomas R. Hall
  1999 Evaluating Cut-Scores on Two Certification Tests: How Well Do Decision Based on Cut-Scores Match teacher- and Principal-Reported Ratings of Competence in the Classroom? Paper presented at the annual meeting of the American Educational Research Association, Montreal, Canada. Georgia Professional Standards Commission, Atlanta.

Quirk, T.J., B.J. Whitten, and S.F. Weinberg
  1973 Review of studies of the concurrent and predictive validity of the National Teacher Examination. *Review of Educational Research* 43:89-114.

Popham, W. James
  1992 Appropriate expectations for content judgments regarding teacher licensure tests. *Applied Measurement in Education* 5(4):285-301.

Pullin, Diana
  1997 Criteria for evaluating teacher tests: A legal perspective. Paper prepared for the National Research Council for the Committee on Assessment and Teacher Quality (September). Boston College, Chestnut Hill, MA.

Richardson v. Lamar County Board of Education, et al., 729 F Supp. 806, 820-21 (M.D. Ala. 1989), aff'd 935 F 2d 1240 (5th Cir.)

Shoho, Alan R., and Nancy K. Martin
  1999 A Comparison of Alienation Among Alternatively and Traditionally Certified Teachers. Paper presented at the meeting of the American Educational Research Association, Montreal, Canada. University of Texas, San Antonio.

Strauss, Robert, and Elizabeth A. Sawyer
    1985   Some new evidence on teacher and student composition. *Economics of Education Review* 5(1):41-48.

Stigler, James W., and James Hiebert
    1999   *The Teaching Gap: Best Ideas from the World's Teachers for Improving Education in the Classroom.* New York: The Free Press.

Society for Industrial and Organizational Psychology
    1987   *Principles for the Validation and Use of Personnel Selection Procedures. Third Edition.* College Park, MD: Society for Industrial and Organizational Psychology.

Turner, Sarah E.
    1999   Who Will Train Teachers? The Changing Degree Output in the Area of Education. Paper presented at the AERA Conference, Montreal, Canada, (April). University of Virginia, Charlottesville.

Wainer, Howard
    1998   *Some comments on the ad hoc committee's critique of the Massachusetts teacher tests.* Education Policy Analysis Archives *7(5):(February 17)*. Available: http://olam.ed.asu.epaa/v7n5.html (3/20/2000).

Biographical Sketches

David Z. Robinson (*Chair*) is a former executive vice president and treasurer of the Carnegie Corporation of New York. He also served as executive director of the Carnegie Commission on Science, Technology, and Government, which recommended improvements in the mechanisms by which the federal and state governments incorporate scientific and technological knowledge in decision making. Prior to joining the Carnegie Corporation, Dr. Robinson worked in the White House as a staff scientist in the Office of the President's Science Advisor and as vice president for academic affairs of New York University, and he has served on several committees of the National Research Council. Dr. Robinson received his Ph.D. in chemical physics from Harvard University.

Andrew Baumgartner is a kindergarten teacher at A. Brian Merry Elementary School in Augusta, GA, and the 1999 National Teacher of the Year. Prior to entering classroom teaching in 1978, Mr. Baumgartner was a speech therapist for the Gilmer County Public Schools. Mr. Baumgartner received his M.A. in early childhood education from North Georgia College.

John T. Bruer is president of the James S. McDonnell Foundation. He established the Cognitive Studies for Educational Practice Program, which supports applications of cognitive science to improve educational outcomes. His book *Schools for Thought: A Science of Learning in the Classroom*, which grew out of the research his program supports, is the basis for a collaboration to develop a research-based curriculum for middle-school students. Dr. Bruer received his Ph.D. in philosophy from the Rockefeller University.

Carl A. Grant is the Hoefs-Bascom professor of teacher education and a professor of Afro-American Studies at the University of Wisconsin-Madison. His research focuses on multicultural education and teacher education, and he is the president of the National Association for Multicultural Education.

Milton D. Hakel is a professor and the Ohio Board of Regents eminent scholar in psychology at Bowling Green State University. His research focuses on leadership development, performance appraisal, job analysis and compensation, and employee selection. He also is president of Organizational Research and Development, Inc., a firm that provides human-resource research consultation. Dr. Hakel received his Ph.D. in psychology from the University of Minnesota.

Linda Darling-Hammond is the Charles E. Ducommun professor of teaching and teacher education at Stanford University, where her research focuses on school restructuring, teacher education, and educational equity. She also is the executive director of the National Commission on Teaching and America's Future, a blue-ribbon panel that has studied policy changes aimed at improving teaching and schooling. She also served as chair of New York State's Council on Curriculum and Assessment and of the Model Standards Committee for the Interstate New Teacher Assessment and Support Consortium. Dr. Darling-Hammond received her Ed.D. in urban education from Temple University.

Abigail L. Hughes is the associate commissioner, division of evaluation and research for the Connecticut State Department of Education. Prior to joining the Connecticut agency, she was a teacher and curriculum coordinator in Ohio and the director of instructional services for a regional service agency in New York State. Dr. Hughes received her M.A. and Ph.D. in educational administration from Ohio State University.

Mary M. Kennedy is a professor in the college of education at Michigan State University, where her research focuses on teacher education and learning. From 1986 through 1993, she directed the National Center for Research on Teacher Learning, a federally funded research center based at Michigan State University. Dr. Kennedy received her Ph.D. in educational psychology from Michigan State University.

Stephen P. Klein is a senior research scientist at the Rand Corporation, where he studies certification and licensing examinations and elementary and secondary educational tests. Dr. Klein served on the NRC's Committee on Appropriate Test Use and the Committee on Education Finance. He received his Ph.D. in industrial psychology from Purdue University.

Catherine Manski is a lecturer and field instructor for English student teachers in the Department of English at the University of Illinois-Chicago. Previously, she was a social studies and English-as-a-second-language teacher at West High School in Madison, WI. Ms. Manski received her M.S. in curriculum and instruction from the University of Wisconsin-Madison.

C. Ford Morishita is a biology teacher at Clackamas High School in Milwaukie, OR and was the 1997 Oregon State Teacher of the Year. He also teaches in the school of education at Portland State University. He received his M.A.T. in biological science from Lewis and Clark College in 1982.

Pamela A. Moss is an associate professor in the school of education at the University of Michigan. Her research focuses on the validity of educational assessments, particularly the assessment of teachers. Dr. Moss serves on the joint committee revising the Standards for Educational and Psychological Testing of the American Educational Research Association, the American Psychological Association, and the National Council of Measurement in Education. She also cochairs the technical advisory committee for the Interstate New Teacher Assessment and Support Consortium, and serves on the Measurement Research Advisory Panel of the National Board for Professional Teaching Standards. Dr. Moss received her Ph.D. in educational research methodology from the University of Pittsburgh.

Barbara S. Plake is director of the Oscar and Luella Buros Center for Testing and the W.C. Meierhenry distinguished university professor at the University of Nebraska-Lincoln. She is the co-editor of the Mental Measurements Yearbook and Applied Measurement in Education. Dr. Plake serves on APA's Committee on Psychological Tests and Assessments. Dr. Plake received her Ph.D. in educational statistics and measurement from the University of Iowa in 1976.

David L. Rose is an attorney in private practice in Washington, D.C., specializing in equal employment opportunity and other employment-related matters. From 1969 through 1987, he was the chief of the Employment Litigation Section of the Civil Rights Division of the Department of Justice, which is responsible for litigation to secure enforcement of laws requiring non-discrimination in employment and equal employment opportunity. Mr. Rose received his L.L.B. from Harvard Law School in 1956.

Robert Rothman (*Study Director*) is a program officer in the Board on Testing and Assessment at the National Research Council. Previously, he was director of special projects for the National Center on Education and the Economy and associate editor of *Education Week*. He is the author of *Measuring Up: Stan-*

dards, Assessment, and School Reform. He has a B.A. from Yale University in political science.

James W. Stigler is a professor of psychology at the University of California, Los Angeles. His research focuses on comparative studies of mathematics teaching and learning among elementary school children in Japan, China, and the United States. Dr. Stigler received his Ph.D. in developmental psychology from the University of Michigan.

Portia Holmes Shields is the president of Albany State University. A former teacher and reading specialist, she also served as the dean of the school of education at Howard University. Dr. Shields received her Ph.D. in early-childhood and elementary education from the University of Maryland at College Park.

Kenneth I. Wolpin is the Lawrence R. Klein professor of economics at the University of Pennsylvania and the director of the University's Institute for Economic Research. His research focuses on life cycle and career decisions of youths. Dr. Wolpin serves on the NRC's Board on Testing and Assessment. He received his Ph.D. in economics from the Graduate School of the City University of New York.